Easy Grammar Grade 3

Student Test Booklet

Wanda C. Phillips

PUBLISHED BY *Easy Grammar Systems*

SCOTTSDALE, ARIZONA 85255

Printed in the United States

© 2006

TABLE OF CONTENTS

TESTS

Name_____

Date_____

A. Sentence Types:
Directions: Place the letter of the sentence type in the blank.

1. _____ Put the cereal away.   A. declarative

2. _____ Yeah! I'm finished!   B. exclamatory

3. _____ Where's your dog?   C. imperative

4. _____ Kim ate a few grapes.   D. interrogative

B. Capitalization:
Directions: Place a capital letter above any word that should be capitalized.

1. on monday, i am going to kaw lake near ponca city.

2. jake asked, "who lives on dale lane?"

3. dear liz,

    is uncle bo driving to long beach on memorial
  day this spring?

        your buddy,

        tate

C. Punctuation:
Directions: Place punctuation where needed (commas, colons, question marks, exclamation points, underlining, and quotation marks).

1. Emily may I help you

2. No we cant leave before 4 00

3. Yikes Im late

4. We met Mr J Cobb on Dec 24 2004

D. Subjects and Verbs:
   Directions: Underline the subject once and the verb or verb phrase twice.
   Note: Crossing out prepositional phrases will help you.

1. Our aunt visits at the end of every summer.

2. After lunch, two boys sat under a tree and talked.

3. My sister and big brother camp in a state park.

4. The shed behind the big barn was struck by a car.

E. Contractions:
   Directions: Write the contraction.

1. are not - _____   3. we are - _____   5. here is - _____

2. who is - _____   4. have not - _____   6. were not - _____

F. Subject-Verb Agreement:
   Directions: Underline the subject once. Underline the verb that agrees twice.
   (Crossing out prepositional phrases will help you.)

1. On the weekends, their dad (bake, bakes).

2. The pastor and his wife (plays, play) tennis.

3. Farmers in that dry area (hope, hopes) for rain.

G. Irregular Verbs:
   Directions: Underline the subject once and the correct verb phrase twice.

1. That team has (chose, chosen) uniforms.

2. He must have (flown, flew) home.

3. A check could be (wrote, written).

4. Pears were (ate, eaten) for a snack.

5. Have you ever (saw, seen) a rattler?

2

6. The river had (rose, risen) two feet.

7. Lanzo should have (took, taken) his father's advice.

H. Tenses:
    Directions: Underline the subject once and the verb or verb phrase twice. Write the tense in the blank.

1. _____ Berry tarts are our dessert.

2. _____ The bell will ring soon.

3. _____ My sister sneezed.

I. Common and Proper Nouns:
    Directions: Circle the common nouns.

1. EMMA   2. DOG   3. POODLE   4. CITY

J. Singular and Plural Nouns:
    Directions: Write the plural of each noun.

1. zebra - _____   5. deer - _____

2. ruby - _____   6. tray - _____

3. mix - _____   7. watch - _____

4. child - _____   8. calf - _____

K. Possessive Nouns:
    Directions: Write the possessive in each blank.

1. a drum that belongs to Ben - _____

2. a corral used by many horses - _____

3. computer belonging to children - _____

L. Identifying Nouns:
    Directions: Circle any nouns.

1. We need to take this shovel, a sleeping bag, two tents, and some strong rope.

M. Conjunctions and Interjections:
    Directions: Draw a box around a conjunction. Circle an interjection.

1. Wow! Jacy won!

2. Give your ticket to my friend or me.

N. Identifying Adjectives:
    Directions: Circle any adjective.

1. Many dirty rags lay on the new carpet.

2. We ordered orange juice and French toast.

O. Degrees of Adjectives:
    Directions: Circle the correct answer.

1. The second pail of water was (sudsier, sudsiest) than the first.

2. Of the five kittens, the gray one is (more playful, most playful).

3. My left foot is (longer, longest) than my right one.

P. Adverbs:
    Directions: Circle adverbs.

1. One child stood up quietly.

2. Peter always goes there with his family.

Q. Degrees of Adverbs:
    Directions: Circle the correct answer.

1. Of the four friends, Tate swims (better, best).

2. Lisa rides her bike (oftener, more often) than her brother.

3. He held the second rope (more tightly, most tightly) than the first rope.

R. Pronouns:
Directions: Circle the correct answer.

1. (She, Her) likes shepherd's pie.

2. Will a bellman take (we, us) to our room?

3. Jacy and (him, he) played checkers.

4. Today, (me and my friend, my friend and me, my friend and I) rode in a taxi.

5. These shells are for (them, they).

6. Mr. Bonds chose (we, us) to hand out posters.

S. Usage:
Directions: Circle the correct answer.

1. I don't feel (good, well).

2. Marco doesn't know (nothing, anything) about it.

3. Do you want to go to the zoo to see (an, a) elephant?

4. The eagles soared high above (its, their) nest.

5. (Your, You're) a great skater!

T. Other Items:

1. Circle the direct object: A boy threw a stone into the stream.

2. Circle the object of the preposition: That man in the dark blue suit is my uncle.

3. Write a regular verb: _____

4. Write an irregular verb: _____

Name_____   **Preposition Test**

Date_____

Directions: Cross out any prepositional phrase(s). Underline the subject once and the verb twice.

Example: Your <u>pillow</u> <u>is</u> ~~under your bed~~.

1.   That baby smiles at his mother.

2.   An eagle soared above our house.

3.   Some sheep came down the country road.

4.   A basket of colored eggs is in the kitchen.

5.   The tired hiker walked through a snowstorm.

6.   On Mondays, Gail goes to the gym.

7.   Karen plays with her brother after school.

8.   During the play, an actor jumped into a box.

9.   Their dad skied between them on the snowy hill.

10. Tina and her husband are from Utah.

11. Before my speech, I looked around the room.

12. The toddler giggled and crawled under the table.

13. Stand beside the Christmas tree for a picture.

14. One of the salesmen hurried across the room.

Date_____

A. Directions: Write the contraction.

1. we are - _____

2. should not - _____

3. I am - _____

4. will not - _____

5. have not - _____

6. they have - _____

7. is not- _____

8. you are - _____

9. I have - _____

10. cannot - _____

11. they are - _____

12. she is - _____

13. has not - _____

14. what is - _____

15. you will - _____

16. here is - _____

B. Directions: Write <u>Yes</u> if the boldfaced verb shows action; write <u>No</u> if the boldfaced verb does not show action.

1. _____   A cow **chews** its cud.
2. _____   Denny **is** a singer.
3. _____   I **stuck** out my tongue.
4. _____   Jenny **sewed** a shirt.
5. _____   Mr. Moss **became** their friend.

C. Directions: Write <u>RV</u> if the verb is a regular verb; write <u>IV</u> if the verb is irregular.

1. _____ to bark   2. _____ to roll   3. _____ to see

D. Directions: Circle the correct verb.

1. He has (swum, swam) in an ocean.

2. Jack must have (drank, drunk) the lemonade.

3. Chimes have (rung, rang) several times.

4. You should have (saw, seen) the parade.

5. Has Dad (went, gone) to work yet?

6. I could have (ate, eaten) more.

7. Tyler had (rode, ridden) his bike.

8. Joy had (flown, flew) to Mexico.

9. The bus has (come, came).

10. His friend must have (brung, brought) chips.

E. Directions: Write <u>can</u> or <u>may</u> on the line.

1. _____ I go to the bathroom?

2. _____ you fasten this for me?

F. Directions: Write the tense of the boldfaced verb or verb phrase.

1. _____ They **will help** you.

2. _____ Ken **found** a dollar.

3. _____ He **answers** the phone on the first ring.

4. _____ Brandy and I **need** a haircut.

10

G. Directions: Circle the correct word.

1. (You're, Your) cat is in a tree.

2. (They're, Their, There) making a playhouse.

3. (They're, Their, There) mom goes to college.

4. That car is missing (it's, its) bumper.

5. I think that (you're, your) wrong.

H. Directions: Circle the verb that agrees with the subject.

1. Three hamsters (live, lives) in that cage.

2. I (add, adds) in my head.

3. Those brothers (do, does) their own washing.

4. One of the babies (cry, cries) after every bath.

5. Jana and Layla (go, goes) to a lake with Aunt Mona.

I. Directions: Cross out any prepositional phrases. Underline the subject
                     once and the verb/verb phrase twice.

1. A woman waded in the lake.

2. The family will eat at a cafe.

3. This road leads to an old barn.

4. She rinsed her hair with lemon juice.

5. Before the meeting, they must have talked for several minutes.   11

Name_____   **Noun Test**

Date_____

A. Directions: Circle the proper noun.

1. country   Canada   2. Mammoth Cave   cave

B. Directions: Circle any nouns.

1. Kelly colored a picture for her grandpa.

2. His shoes and socks are under the bed.

C. Directions: Write the plural.

1. doughnut - _____   5. story -_____

2. half - _____   6. tomato - _____

3. key -_____   7. foot - _____

4. deer - _____   8. latch - _____

D. Directions: Write the possessive.

1. balloons belonging to one girl - _____

2. balloons belonging to more than one girl - _____

3. a book owned by one child - _____

4. a book shared by more than one child - _____

A. Directions: Cross out the prepositional phrase in each sentence.
Then, underline the subject once and the verb twice.

1. I ate two bowls of cereal.

2. A paper and crayons are on the floor.

3. Mrs. Jones washed two spoons and dried them.

4. Do you want an ice cream cone?

5. Hold this for me.

B. Directions: Write the contraction in the space provided.

1. we have - _____   4. they will - _____

2. I am - _____   5. she is - _____

3. has not - _____   6. should not - _____

C. Directions: Circle the correct word.

1. (It's, Its) a very sad story.

2. (You're, Your) dad is here for you.

3. (They're, There, Their) planning a camping trip.

4. (Can, May) I help you?

5. I know (they're, there, their) grandmother.   15

D. Directions: Write <u>Yes</u> if the boldfaced verb shows action. Write <u>No</u> if the boldfaced verb does not show action.

1. _____   Rob **paddles** a canoe.

2. _____   An ostrich **is** a fast bird.

E. Directions: Write <u>RV</u> if the verb is regular and <u>IV</u> if the verb is irregular.

1. _____ to do   2. _____ to walk

F. Directions: Circle the correct verb.

1. Dad must have (ate, eaten) all of the chips.

2. Lenny has (went, gone) to a horse show.

3. The child should have (gave, given) me the note.

4. A fork had (fallen, fell) into the trash.

G. Directions: Write the tense (*present, past,* or *future*) of the boldfaced verb.

1. _____   He **will** not **stop**.

2. _____   Jana and Jody **are** twins.

3. _____   The car **stopped** suddenly.

H. Directions: Circle the correct verb.

1. My sister and I (wants, want) dessert.

2. A rose (opens, open) slowly.

3. They always (drink, drinks) milk for lunch.

16

Name_____

Date_____

A. Directions: Write <u>a</u> or <u>an</u> before each word.

1. _____ orange   3. _____ apple   5. _____ eye

2. _____ pancake   4. _____ tent   6. _____ umbrella

B. Directions: Circle each adjective.

1. A few wild geese flew over the lake.

2. The old house needs a new roof.

3. Brent likes mystery books and animal stories.

4. Three young girls rode small ponies.

5. The young woman ordered an egg sandwich.

C. Directions: Circle the correct form.

1. The green jello is (more firm, firmer) than the red jello.

2. Joyann is the (shorter, shortest) twin.

3. His red car was the (cleaner, cleanest) one in the parking lot.

4. The second test was (badder, worse) than the first one.

5. Of all the pictures in the album, Grandma's wedding picture is (lovelier, loveliest).

Name_____ **Cumulative Test**
                                                Adjectives
Date_____

A. Directions: Cross out the prepositional phrase in each sentence.
                     Then, underline the subject once and the verb twice.

1.   A fox lives in that hole.

2.   Two cars and a truck pulled into the driveway.

3.   Put the broom by the back door.

4.   Did you write your name above the date?

5.   Craig packed boxes and set them on a wagon.

B. Directions: Write the contraction in the space provided.

1.   I will - _____   4.   we are - _____

2.   is not - _____   5.   cannot - _____

3.   what is - _____   6.   they are - _____

C. Directions: Circle the correct word.

1.   I don't know if (it's, its) time to eat.

2.   (You're, Your) a good basketball player.

3.   (They're, There, Their) not ready.

4.   You (can, may) get a drink.

5.   Cassie and Dora want to bring (they're, there, their) dog along.

D. Directions: Write <u>Yes</u> if the boldfaced verb shows action. Write <u>No</u> if the boldfaced verb does not show action.

1. _____   Heidi **swings** the bat too soon.

2. _____   This bread **tastes** stale.

E. Directions: Circle the correct verb.

1. The hamster (runs, run) around in its cage.

2. Roses (bloom, blooms) for many months.

3. Ned and I (hike, hikes) nearly every Saturday.

F. Directions: Write <u>RV</u> if the verb is regular and <u>IV</u> if the verb is irregular.

1. _____ to find   2. _____ to live   3. _____ to join

G. Directions: Underline the verb phrase twice.
    Reminder: Underlining the subject once may help you to find the verb phrase.

1. They had chosen white roses for their wedding.

2. These crackers are broken into many pieces.

3. I have not received my package.

H. Directions: Circle the correct verb.

1. She has (wrote, written) us a note.

2. That business has (given, give) coupons to its best customers.

20

3.   The ladies have (shaken, shook) hands.

4.   Several toys had been (broke, broken).

5.   They had (drank, drunk) too much lemonade.

6.   She has (sung, sang) for our President.

7.   Her keys had been (stole, stolen).

8.   You should have (brang, brought) your video games.

9.   Miss Jones has (rode, ridden) in a helicopter.

10.   Which was (chosen, chose) as the winner?

I. Directions: Write the tense (*present, past,* or *future*) of the boldfaced verb.

1. _____   Loran often **sleeps** in a tent.

2. _____   Both horses **galloped** fast.

3. _____   He **will pick** you up at the airport.

4. _____   They **gather** firewood each fall.

J. Directions: Write <u>C</u> if the noun is common. Write <u>P</u> if the noun is proper.

1. _____ CITY   3. _____ DALLAS

2. _____ NEWSPAPER   4. _____ CANARY

K. Directions: Write the plural of each noun.

1. pass - _____   6. friend - _____

2. pan - _____   7. bee - _____

3. lady - _____   8. eyelash -_____

4. tomato - _____   9. elf - _____

5. child - _____   10. ray - _____

L. Directions: Write the possessive.

1.   a book belonging to Hannah - _____

2.   a room shared by two boys - _____

3.   a meeting held for more than one man - _____

4.   checkers belonging to Chris - _____

M. Directions: Circle any nouns in each sentence.

1. A motorcycle is sitting in the driveway.

2. Jerry put milk in his bowl of cereal.

3. Several babies slept on towels at the beach.

4. A policeman raised his hand and blew his whistle.

Name_____   **Adverb Test**

Date_____

A. Directions: Circle the adverb that tells **how**:

1. The car stopped suddenly.

2. Beth kicks the soccer ball hard.

B. Directions: Circle the adverb that tells **when**:

1. I'll do that later.

2. Now, let's decide.

C. Directions: Circle the adverb that tells **where**:

1. I can't find my brush anywhere.

2. Please come in.

D. Directions: Circle the adverb that tells **to what extent**:

1. Our trash is quite full.

2. This book is very interesting.

E. Directions: Circle the correct adverb form.

1. The small monkey chatters (more noisily, most noisily) than the larger one.

2. Brian swam (faster, fastest) in his third lap.

3. Grandpa comes to the park (more often, oftener) than his friend.

Name_____   **Pronoun Test**

Date_____

A. Directions: Circle the correct pronoun.

1.   His team played against (we, us).

2.   (She, Her) has come alone.

3.   Their mother sat beside (I, me).

4.   Miss Plank tutors (they, them) on Saturday.

5.   At the end of June, (we, us) go to a baseball camp.

6.   His partner told (he, him) about the case.

7.   (They, Them) have bought hot dogs for lunch.

8.   Jill and (me, I) want to take piano lessons.

9.   Are the cookies from (she, her)?

10.   Between innings, Roy and (he, him) walked around.

B.   Directions: Circle the correct word.

1.   Someone said that (its, it's) beginning to snow.

2.   Are the windows in (your, you're) van rolled down?

3.   The Hunts take (their, they're, there) dogs to the park.

4.   (Your, You're) the first to hear the news.

5.   Don't stop them. (Their, They're, There) in a hurry.   25

A.   Directions: Cross out any prepositional phrase(s). Underline the
                     subject once and the verb or verb phrase twice.
                     Label the direct object - D.O. in sentences 4, 5, and 6.

1.   Herb works on a farm during the summer.

2.   Daisies and roses have been placed in a vase.

3.   Step into the tub of warm water.

4.   Todd sands and paints furniture for his uncle.

5.   We could not attend the wedding.

6.   Rita must have given her ring to her sister.

B.   Directions: Circle the correct verb.

1.   He (can, may) dive well.

2.   You (can, may) check out this library book.

3.   (Can, May) Mrs. Storm take your coat?

4.   His posters (shine, shines) in the dark.

5.   A bear (lives, live) in those woods.

6.   I (clean, cleans) my room each week.

7.   Jay and his sister (like, likes) to sled.

C. Directions: Write the contraction.

1. I am - _____   8. are not - _____

2. that is - _____   9. who is - _____

3. you will - _____   10. will not - _____

4. would not - _____   11. cannot - _____

5. they are - _____   12. we are - _____

6. she is - _____   13. is not - _____

7. does not - _____   14. I will - _____

D. Directions: Write <u>Yes</u> if the boldfaced verb shows action. Write <u>No</u> if the boldfaced verb does not show action.

1. _____   Her book **fell** to the floor.

2. _____   I **feel** sick.

3. _____   A large owl often **sits** on that branch.

E. Directions: Write <u>RV</u> in the blank if the verb is regular. Write <u>IV</u> if the verb is irregular.

1. _____ to speak   2. _____ to crawl   3. _____ to keep

F. Directions: Circle the correct verb.

1.   The dam has (busted, burst).

2.   I could have (swum, swam) longer.

3.   Have you ever (ran, run) in a relay race?

4.   Jude must have (stole, stolen) third base!

5.   I have never (seen, saw) a puffin.

6.   Has the telephone (rang, rung)?

7.   You should have (rode, ridden) your bike.

8.   Shirley may not have (taken, took) the right bus.

9.   He has (went, gone) to a movie with his dad.

10.   Someone must have (drunk, drank) my milk.

G.   Directions: Write the tense (*present*, *past*, or *future*) of the boldfaced verb.

1.   _____   I **hid** your present.

2.   _____   Jimmy **saves** pennies.

3.   _____   Ken **will type** his paper tomorrow.

4.   _____   They sometimes **sleep** outside.

Cumulative Test
Pronouns

A.   Directions: Write <u>C</u> if the noun is common. Write <u>P</u> if the noun is proper.

1. _____ RIVER   3. _____ GLENN   5. _____ BUILDING

2. _____ SNAKE RIVER   4. _____ BOY   6. _____ TOWER

B.   Directions: Write the plural.

1. match - _____   6. play - _____

2. guppy - _____   7. deer - _____

3. eye - _____   8. mouse - _____

4. rash - _____   9. box - _____

5. child - _____   10. tomato - _____

C.   Directions: Circle any nouns.

1.   The man carried a stick and a cane.

2.   Derek baked brownies and cookies.

3.   Her parents visited friends in Texas.

4.   Does Ginger have a ticket for the show?

31

D.   Directions: Write the possessive.

1.   a car belonging to Nancy - _____

2.   a room shared by two boys - _____

3.   the president of a club - _____

4.   a swing used by more than one child - _____

E.   Directions: Circle any adjectives.

1.   The lynx is an animal with a short tail.

2.   A dolphin has a long body and many teeth.

3.   Latina has straight red hair and big blue eyes.

4.   I ate two juicy plums and several sour grapes.

F.   Directions: Circle the correct form.

1.   This bat is the (lighter, lightest) of the three.

2.   Your dad is (quieter, quietest) than your mom.

3.   Of all the children, Andy is (more loving, most loving).

4.   Is a cobra (more harmful, most harmful) than a rattlesnake?

A.   Directions: Write <u>conj.</u> above each conjunction.
                     Write <u>intj.</u> above each interjection.

1.   Yippee! Vicki or Luke finished first!

2.   Brook and her son left, but they forgot their cards.

B.   Directions: Write the sentence type.

Remember: A **declarative** sentence makes a *statement.*
                    An **interrogative** sentence asks a *question.*
                    An **imperative** sentence gives a *command.*
                    An **exclamatory** sentence *shows emotion.*

1.   _____   A panda lives in China.

2.   _____   Let's go!

3.   _____   What do you want?

4.   _____   Please put this in your room.

C.   Directions: Circle the adverb that tells *how.*

1.   The boy fell limply across his bed.

2.   Her aunt talked excitedly about her trip.

3.   Mr. and Mrs. Scribber bowl well.

D. Directions: Circle the adverb that tells *when*.

1. I'll catch up with you later.

2. First, I must close the door.

3. Yesterday, Bruce visited his uncle.

4. What happened then?

E. Directions: Circle the adverb that tells *where*.

1. The dog wants to go out.

2. Have you seen Laura anywhere?

3. I want to stay home.

F. Directions: Circle the adverb that tells *to what extent*.

1. The man was too sleepy to drive.

2. That comic strip is so funny.

3. You're very welcome.

G. Directions: Circle the correct form.

1. Sam runs (faster, fastest) in his neighborhood.

2. She looked (more closely, most closely) at the third picture.

3. I drive (more slowly, most slowly) than my son.

4. His thumb was hurt (more seriously, most seriously) than his index finger.

Name_____   **Capitalization Test**

Date_____

Directions: Write the capital letter above any word that needs to be
               capitalized.

1.   is whitefish lake in minnesota?

2.   last sunday, i took my dogs to riverside park.

3.   his new address will be 2 west ash lane.

4.   kamet mountain is in the country of india.

5.   franco will attend sunset middle school in august.

6.   william a. chase works for hampton shoe company.

7.   dena said, "you'll want to visit ozark national forest."

8.   the betsy ross house is in the city of philadelphia.

9.   did aunt ali make cherry cake for valentine's day?

10.   these two lines of poetry were in my english book:
          mama's shiny purple coat
          giant-sized shoulder bag to tote

11. dear rick,

        tonight, our family will go sailing on the pacific ocean.

                              friends forever,

                              brody

12.   mom found a book named <u>the best of baking</u> at buckeye library.

35

Name_____   **Punctuation Test**

Date_____

Directions: Use needed punctuation.

Remember: You have learned about periods, apostrophes, commas, colons, question marks, exclamation points, underlining, and quotation marks.

1.   Please dont sit there

2.   Yes the time is 9 30

3.   Wow We won a prize

4.   Marys room is painted blue

5.   Her home is near the Green Mts in Vermont

6.   He read the book named Top Wing

7.   Bobby may I borrow your skates

8.   They were married on Nov 18 1996

9.   Dear Liz

         I found your camera in our car

                  Your friend

                  Rich

10.   His favorite short story is The Snow in Chelm

Date_____

A. Sentence Types:
   Directions: Place the letter of the sentence type in the blank.

1. _____ Put the cereal away.   A. declarative

2. _____ Yeah! I'm finished!   B. exclamatory

3. _____ Where's your dog?   C. imperative

4. _____ Kim ate a few grapes.   D. interrogative

B. Capitalization:
   Directions: Place a capital letter above any word that should be capitalized.

1. on monday, i am going to kaw lake near ponca city.

2. jake asked, "who lives on dale lane?"

3. dear liz,

   is uncle bo driving to long beach on memorial

   day this spring?

                    your buddy,

                    tate

C. Punctuation:
   Directions: Place punctuation where needed (commas, colons, question marks, exclamation points, underlining, and quotation marks).

1. Emily may I help you

2. No we cant leave before 4 00

3. Yikes Im late

4. We met Mr J Cobb on Dec 24 2004

D. Subjects and Verbs:
     Directions: Underline the subject once and the verb or verb phrase twice.
                       Note: Crossing out prepositional phrases will help you.

1.   Our aunt visits at the end of every summer.

2.   After lunch, two boys sat under a tree and talked.

3.   My sister and big brother camp in a state park.

4.   The shed behind the big barn was struck by a car.

E. Contractions:
     Directions: Write the contraction.

1.   are not - _____   3. we are - _____   5. here is - _____

2.   who is - _____   4. have not - _____   6. were not - _____

F. Subject-Verb Agreement:
     Directions: Underline the subject once. Underline the verb that agrees twice.
                       (Crossing out prepositional phrases will help you.)

1.   On the weekends, their dad (bake, bakes).

2.   The pastor and his wife (plays, play) tennis.

3.   Farmers in that dry area (hope, hopes) for rain.

G. Irregular Verbs:
     Directions: Underline the subject once and the correct verb phrase twice.

1.   That team has (chose, chosen) uniforms.

2.   He must have (flown, flew) home.

3.   A check could be (wrote, written).

4.   Pears were (ate, eaten) for a snack.

5.   Have you ever (saw, seen) a rattler?

40

6. The river had (rose, risen) two feet.

7. Lanzo should have (took, taken) his father's advice.

H. Tenses:
   Directions: Underline the subject once and the verb or verb phrase twice. Write the tense in the blank.

1. _____ Berry tarts are our dessert.

2. _____ The bell will ring soon.

3. _____ My sister sneezed.

I. Common and Proper Nouns:
   Directions: Circle the common nouns.

1. EMMA   2. DOG   3. POODLE   4. CITY

J. Singular and Plural Nouns:
   Directions: Write the plural of each noun.

1. zebra - _____   5. deer - _____

2. ruby - _____   6. tray - _____

3. mix - _____   7. watch - _____

4. child - _____   8. calf - _____

K. Possessive Nouns:
   Directions: Write the possessive in each blank.

1. a drum that belongs to Ben - _____

2. a corral used by many horses - _____

3. computer belonging to children - _____

L. Identifying Nouns:
    Directions: Circle any nouns.

1. We need to take this shovel, a sleeping bag, two tents, and some strong rope.

M. Conjunctions and Interjections:
    Directions: Draw a box around a conjunction. Circle an interjection.

1. Wow! Jacy won!

2. Give your ticket to my friend or me.

N. Identifying Adjectives:
    Directions: Circle any adjective.

1. Many dirty rags lay on the new carpet.

2. We ordered orange juice and French toast.

O. Degrees of Adjectives:
    Directions: Circle the correct answer.

1. The second pail of water was (sudsier, sudsiest) than the first.

2. Of the five kittens, the gray one is (more playful, most playful).

3. My left foot is (longer, longest) than my right one.

P. Adverbs:
    Directions: Circle adverbs.

1. One child stood up quietly.

2. Peter always goes there with his family.

Q. Degrees of Adverbs:
    Directions: Circle the correct answer.
1. Of the four friends, Tate swims (better, best).

2. Lisa rides her bike (oftener, more often) than her brother.

3. He held the second rope (more tightly, most tightly) than the first rope.

R. Pronouns:
   Directions: Circle the correct answer.

1. (She, Her) likes shepherd's pie.

2. Will a bellman take (we, us) to our room?

3. Jacy and (him, he) played checkers.

4. Today, (me and my friend, my friend and me, my friend and I) rode in a taxi.

5. These shells are for (them, they).

6. Mr. Bonds chose (we, us) to hand out posters.

S. Usage:
   Directions: Circle the correct answer.

1. I don't feel (good, well).

2. Marco doesn't know (nothing, anything) about it.

3. Do you want to go to the zoo to see (an, a) elephant?

4. The eagles soared high above (its, their) nest.

5. (Your, You're) a great skater!

T. Other Items:

1. Circle the direct object: A boy threw a stone into the stream.

2. Circle the object of the preposition: That man in the dark blue suit is my uncle.

3. Write a regular verb: _____

4. Write an irregular verb: _____

Reflections

Preposition Test

_____

_____

_____

_____

_____

_____

_____

_____

_____

_____

_____

_____

Reflections

Verb Test

_____

_____

_____

_____

_____

_____

_____

_____

_____

_____

_____

_____

Reflections

Noun Test

_____

_____

_____

_____

_____

_____

_____

_____

_____

_____

_____

_____

_____

Reflections

Adjective Test

_____

_____

_____

_____

_____

_____

_____

_____

_____

_____

_____

Reflections

Adverb Test

_____

_____

_____

_____

_____

_____

_____

_____

_____

_____

_____

_____

_____

Reflections

Pronoun Test

_____

_____

_____

_____

_____

_____

_____

_____

_____

_____

_____

_____

Reflections

Capitalization Test

_____

_____

_____

_____

_____

_____

_____

_____

_____

_____

_____

Reflections

Punctuation Test

_____

_____

_____

_____

_____

_____

_____

_____

_____

_____

_____

Reflections

Cumulative Test: Nouns

_____

_____

_____

_____

_____

_____

_____

_____

_____

_____

_____

Reflections

Cumulative Test: Adjectives

_____

_____

_____

_____

_____

_____

_____

_____

_____

_____

_____

Reflections

Cumulative Test: Pronouns

_____

_____

_____

_____

_____

_____

_____

_____

_____

_____

_____

_____